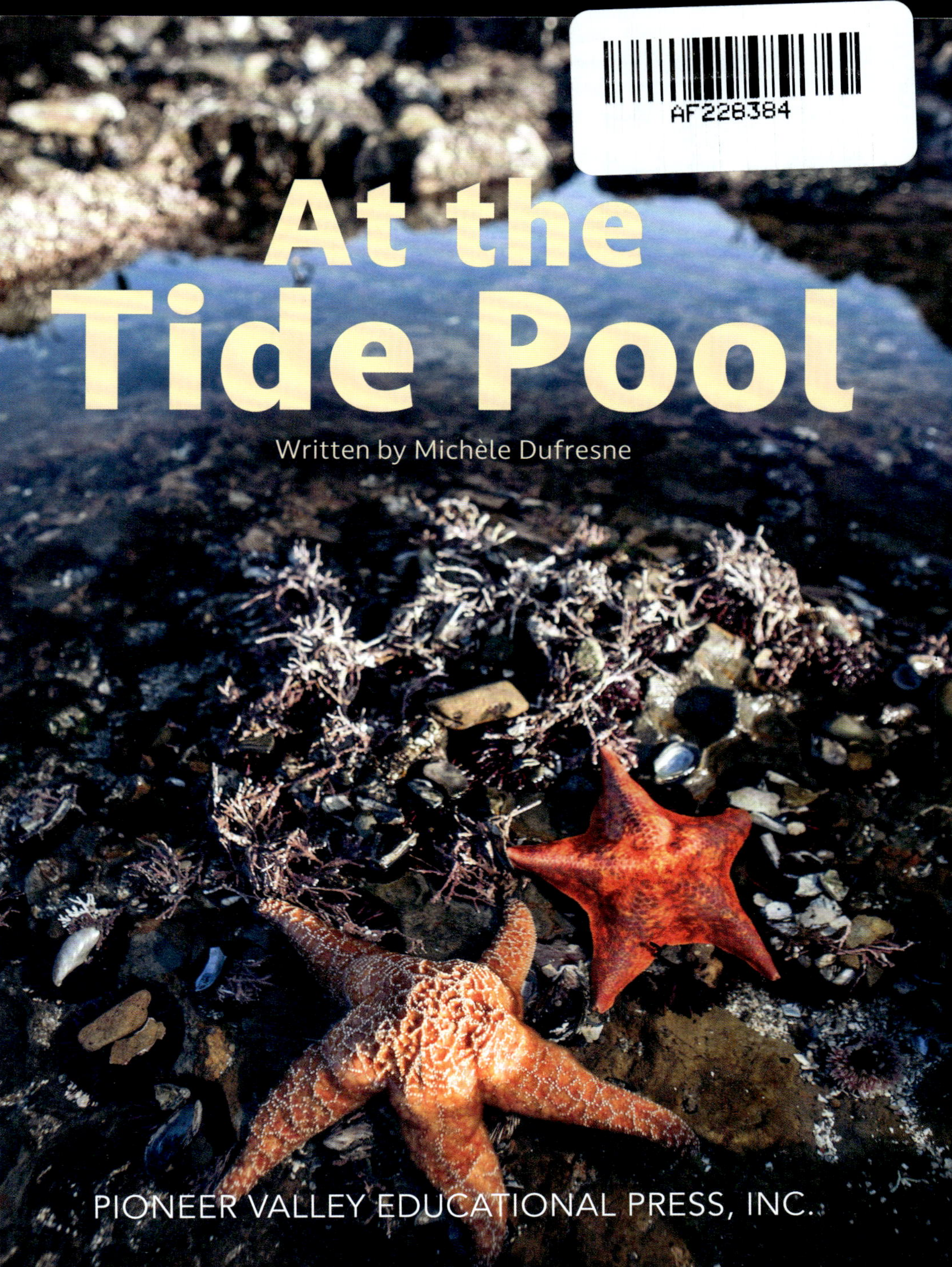

At the Tide Pool

Written by Michèle Dufresne

PIONEER VALLEY EDUCATIONAL PRESS, INC.

A **tide pool** is a small pool of **seawater**. As the waves come in with the tide, seawater fills holes and cracks in the rocks.

When the waves go back out, seawater gets stuck and makes a tide pool. Many **animals** and plants get stuck in the pool.

The tide pool is home to many animals. Animals that live in the small pools must cope with waves that rush into their homes. They also must cope with the sun that blazes down and makes the seawater hot.

Tide pools are like mini oceans. Animals that live in them must survive waves, the hot sun, and limited space!

Here is a **sea star**.

Sea stars are not fish.

Most sea stars have five **arms**.

You can find many sea stars

in tide pools.

Can you see the white bumps on the sea star?

These bumps are spines. The spines help keep the sea star safe from **predators**.

Sea stars have hundreds of tube feet. They use their feet to move around and to capture prey.

Here are some clams.

The shells on clams keep them safe

from the waves that crash

on the rocks.

The shells also keep them safe

from predators.

Here is a crab. It also has a shell.

The crab clings to a rock

as the wave rolls in.

Shore crabs are scavengers. They keep tide pools clean by eating bits of food left behind by other animals.

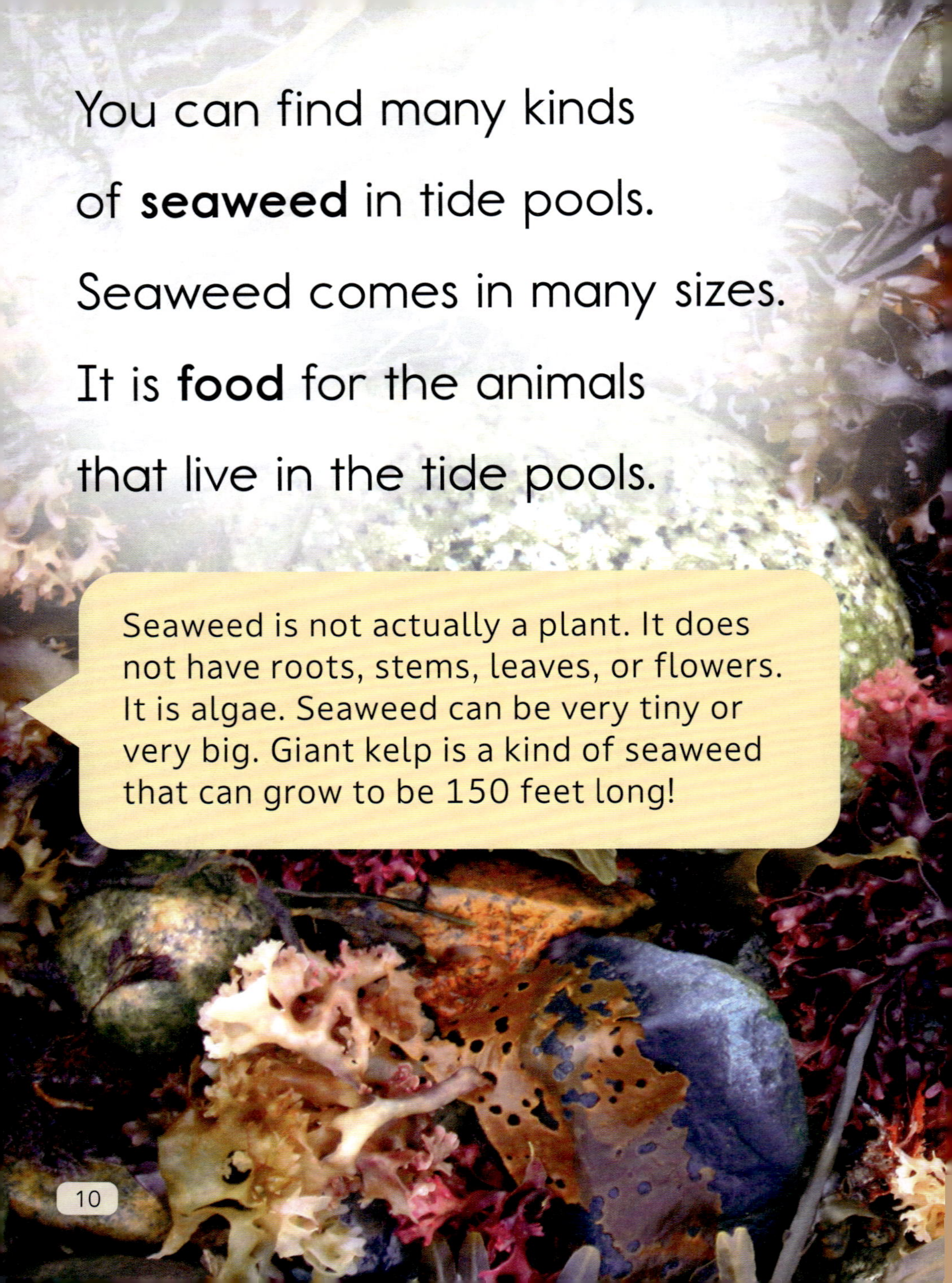

You can find many kinds
of **seaweed** in tide pools.

Seaweed comes in many sizes.

It is **food** for the animals

that live in the tide pools.

Seaweed is not actually a plant. It does not have roots, stems, leaves, or flowers. It is algae. Seaweed can be very tiny or very big. Giant kelp is a kind of seaweed that can grow to be 150 feet long!

glossary

animals:
living things
that move,
eat, and grow

food:
something
animals eat to
stay alive
and strong

sea star:
a sea animal
with arms that
lives on rocks;
also called
a starfish

seaweed:
a type of algae
that grows in
the ocean and
on rocks

arms:
extensions of
the body

predators:
animals that
hunt and eat
other animals

seawater:
salt water from
the ocean

tide pool:
a small pool of
ocean water
left behind
when the tide
goes out